This collection of atoms certifies

as an official

MinuteEarthling

MinuteEarth EXPLAINS

HOW DID WHALES GET SO BIG?

And Other Curious Questions about Animals, Nature, Geology, and Planet Earth

Written and Illustrated by MinuteEarth

Dragon Fruit

Published by DragonFruit, an imprint of Mango Publishing,
a division of Mango Publishing Group, Inc.
2850 Douglas Road 2nd Floor
Coral Gables, FL 33134
www.mangopublishinggroup.com

MinuteEarth Explains: How Did Whales Get So Big?
And Other Curious Questions about Animals, Nature, Geology, and Planet Earth

ISBN: (p) 978-1-64250-631-0 (e) 978-1-64250-632-7
LCCN: 2021934495
BISAC: JNF037010, JUVENILE

NONFICTION / Science & Nature / Earth Sciences / Earthquakes & Volcanoes.

Printed in the United States of America.

Written by Emily Elert, David Goldenberg, Alex Reich, Henry Reich,
Peter Reich, and Kate Yoshida.

Edited by Kate Yoshida and Natasha Vera.

Illustrated by Ever Salazar with contributions by Arcadi Garcia Rius,
Sarah J. Berman, Qingyang Chen, Omkar Bhagat, and Jessika Raisor.

Cover designed by Arcadi Garcia Rius and Sarah J. Berman.
Interior designed by Sarah J. Berman.

Additional contributions by Julián Gustavo Gómez, Melissa Hayes,
and countless other writers, editors, and experts.

The text face is Futura, designed by Paul Renner.
The titling face is Si Kancil, designed by Adien Gunarta.

MIX
Paper from
responsible sources
FSC® C005010
www.fsc.org

FIRST EDITION

Remember...you're part of something big.

CONTENTS

INTRODUCTION

Human beings (including you!) are incredibly curious creatures. For as long as we have existed, we have been trying to figure out how our planet works—not just to solve problems we have encountered, but also to satisfy our endless curiosity. Along the way, we have discovered countless amazing things about the world around us.

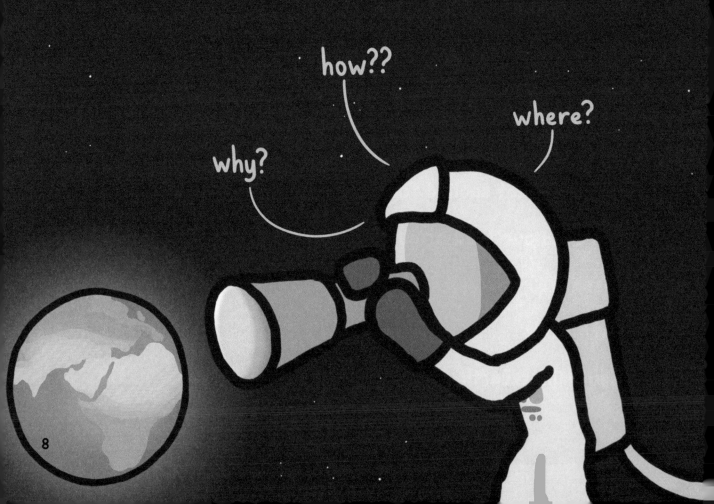

In this book, we'll share just a few of those amazing things with you. Some of the questions in this collection are ones you may already have wondered—like why do leaves turn such dazzling colors in the fall? Others are a little wackier—like if a wool sweater shrinks in the wash, why don't sheep shrink in the rain? Each of the answers provides a fun peek into the intricate and interconnected workings of our wonderful planet.

Welcome to
MinuteEarth!

PSST!
You can find definitions for **bolded** key words
in the glossary at the end of the book.

Where did Earth's water come from?

Unlike every other planet in our solar system, Earth's surface is 70% liquid water. That's useful for sustaining life, but it's also weird because our planet didn't start off with water.

The early **inner solar system** was far too hot for frozen water, and any water vapor would have been blasted away by the solar wind.

So how did we end up with such splendid oceans, rivers, ice caps, and clouds?

Natural processes like burning and breathing do create water through chemical reactions, but other natural processes, like **photosynthesis**, use up that water. Plus, these amounts are so tiny that we can be confident that Earth's water wasn't made here over the eons.

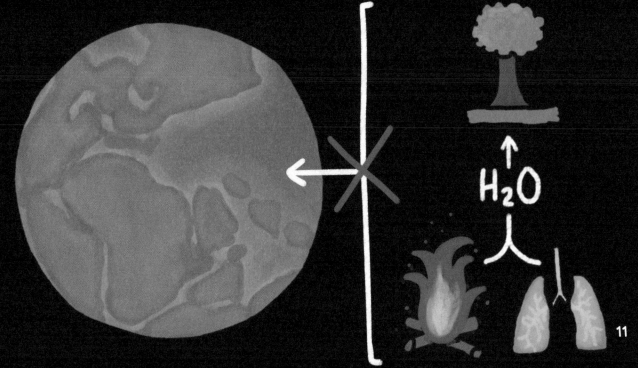

H_2O

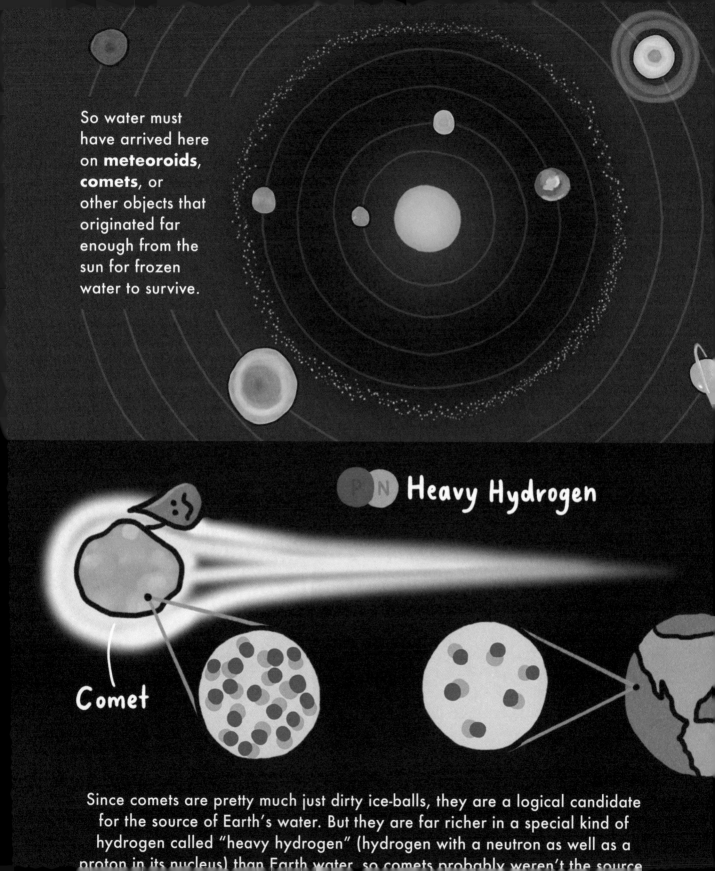

So water must have arrived here on **meteoroids**, **comets**, or other objects that originated far enough from the sun for frozen water to survive.

Heavy Hydrogen

Comet

Since comets are pretty much just dirty ice-balls, they are a logical candidate for the source of Earth's water. But they are far richer in a special kind of hydrogen called "heavy hydrogen" (hydrogen with a neutron as well as a proton in its nucleus) than Earth water, so comets probably weren't the source

The more likely source is a kind of stony **meteorite** known as a "carbonaceous chondrite." These meteoroids form far enough from the sun that they can hold water—and the water they do have has similar levels of heavy hydrogen as Earth's water.

So it seems as though the water that turned our planet into a blue marble came, quite literally, out of the blue.

Why do rivers curve?

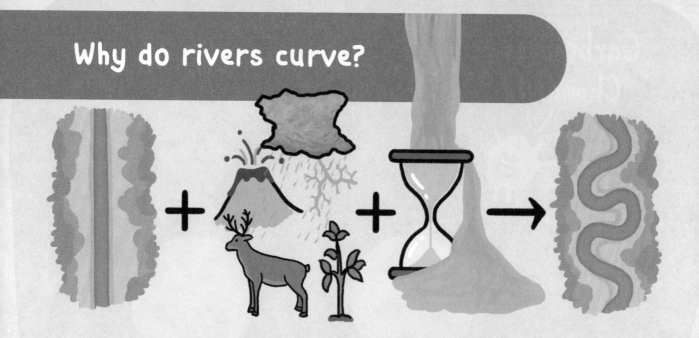

All it takes to turn a straight stretch of river into a bendy one is a little disturbance and a lot of time—and in nature, there's plenty of both.

Say, for example, a muskrat burrows into the bank of a stream. Her tunnels make a cozy home, but they also weaken the bank, which begins to crumble.

1

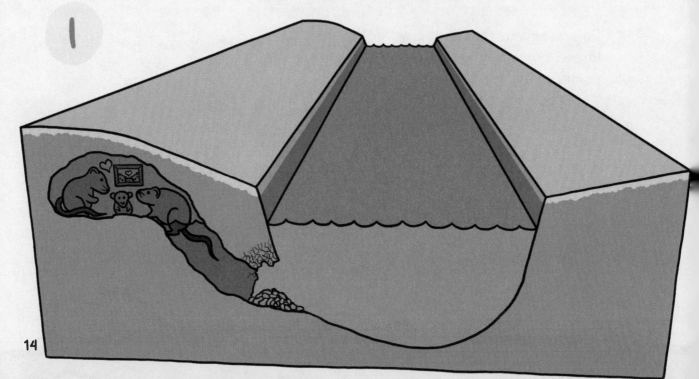

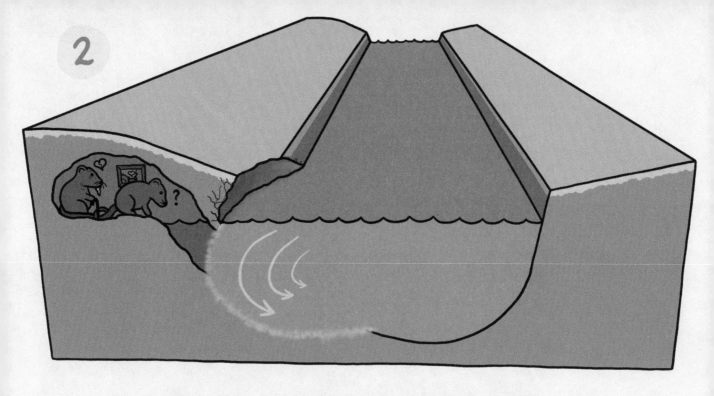

Water rushes in, sweeping away loose dirt and making the hollow even hollower, which lets the water rush a little faster and sweep away a little more dirt...and so on.

As more water flows into the deepening hole, the flow near the opposite bank weakens and slows. And since slow-moving water can't carry as much dirt as fast-moving water can, dirt starts building up on the inside bank.

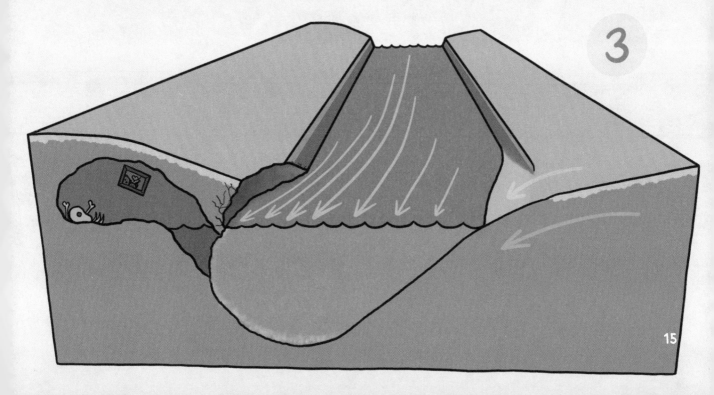

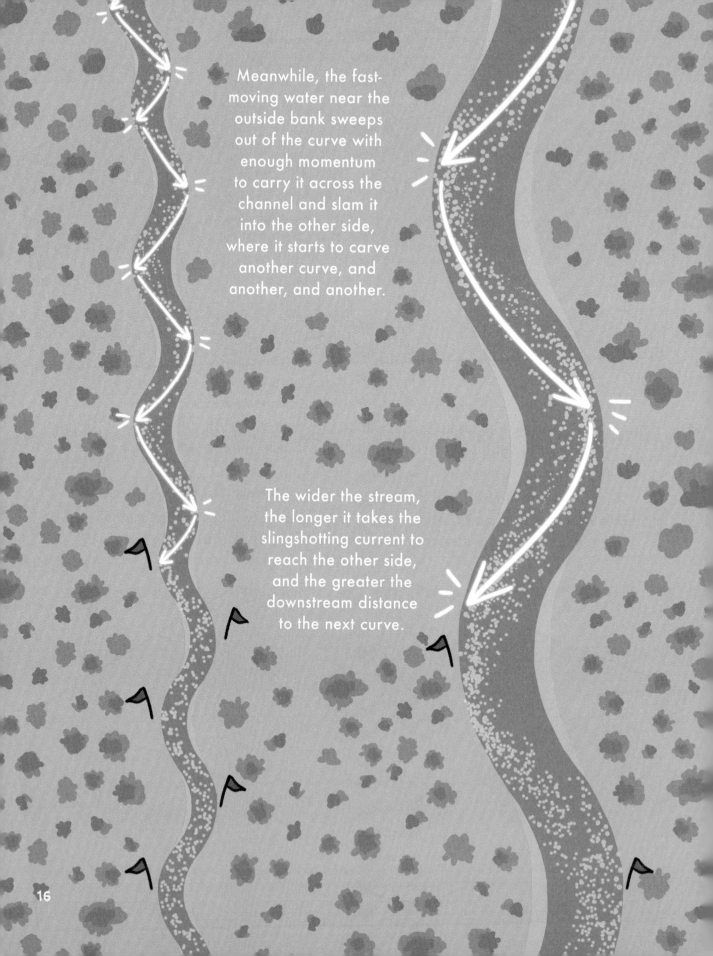

Meanwhile, the fast-moving water near the outside bank sweeps out of the curve with enough momentum to carry it across the channel and slam it into the other side, where it starts to carve another curve, and another, and another.

The wider the stream, the longer it takes the slingshotting current to reach the other side, and the greater the downstream distance to the next curve.

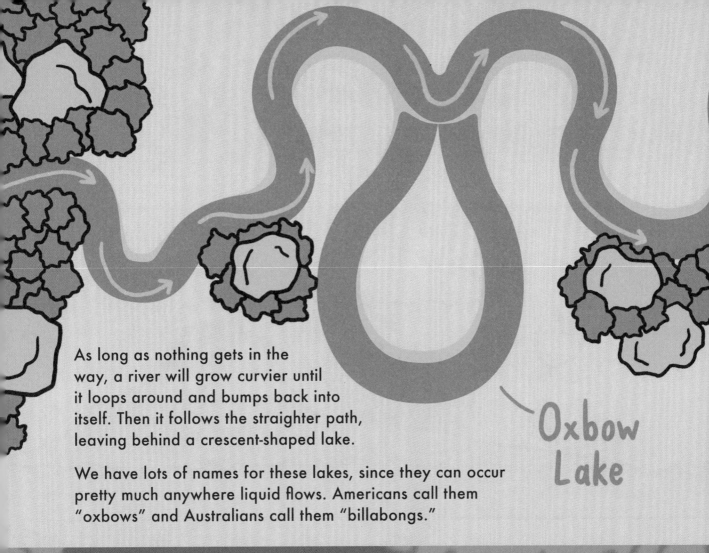

As long as nothing gets in the way, a river will grow curvier until it loops around and bumps back into itself. Then it follows the straighter path, leaving behind a crescent-shaped lake.

We have lots of names for these lakes, since they can occur pretty much anywhere liquid flows. Americans call them "oxbows" and Australians call them "billabongs."

Oxbow Lake

00111111
00100001

But that brings up an interesting question: what do the Martians call the ancient ones on Mars?

?

Which came first: the rain or the rainforest?

The Hawaiian proverb "hahai no ka ua i ka ulula'au" means "the rain follows after the forest." But wait...since all plants need water, shouldn't the forest follow after the rain? Well, it turns out that both are true.

During photosynthesis, land plants open the pores on their leaves to grab carbon dioxide for making energy. But they also lose water through these open pores, which in turn draws more water up through their stems.

Trees that live in the rainforest can afford to keep those pores open— and photosynthesize a lot— because there is plenty of water in the soil that they can use and lose.

And all that lost water rises up from the forest in the form of water vapor, feeding clouds and accelerating the formation of rain. The rain falls to the ground and gets taken up all over again.

So without the forest pumping so much water into the air, rainforests wouldn't be as rainy. And without so much rain, the forest couldn't pump so much water into the air. But how did this cycle get started in the first place?

Well, long before rainforests, ancestors of trees like cypress, pine, and spruce dominated the land. But these plants didn't use—or lose—much water, so the air tended to be dry, with less rain.

Gymnosperms

Then around 130 million years ago, a new kind of plant took the risk of losing more water in return for souped-up photosynthesis. These were **angiosperms**—flowering plants—and their risk paid off: faster growth enabled them to take over the planet's tropical regions.

Angiosperms

Angiosperms pumped so much water into the air that,
as they spread, they brought their own rain with them.

So it's true, "hahai no ka ua i ka ulula'au."
And once the rain has followed after the forest,
the forest follows after the rain, and so on and so on.

Can fighting wildfires make them worse?

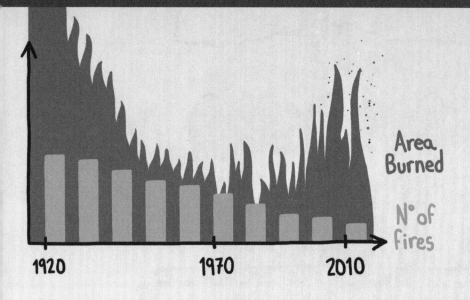

Area Burned

N° of fires

1920   1970   2010

The number of wildfires each year in the US has been decreasing since 1920. But since just 1970, the total area burned each year has more than doubled. That seems weird—if we're seeing fewer fires, why is there more damage?

The answer is largely that we've been fighting more fires. Stopping forests from burning leads to denser forests packed with flammable needles and dry branches of dead or dying trees.

So the average forest fire today burns hotter, bigger, and faster than it used to.

What's more, wildfires will keep getting harder to tame as climate change turns forests hotter and drier, and as homes edge further into fire-prone areas.

The good news is that we can prevent future wildfires from getting so wild by taming their fuel supply. Essentially, this means letting some wildfires burn (or even starting them ourselves) when conditions aren't too dry or windy, or cutting down some trees to make the forests less crowded.

When and where we've used it, this strategy has made fires cooler, slower, and less destructive.

For instance, when a blaze ripped through Washington State in 2006, untamed areas lost 92% of their trees, while just 49% of trees burned in places recently thinned by cutting and controlled burns.

Unmanaged

Managed

So far, it has been tough to convince people—and the government—that by deliberately burning some forests we can save way more.

But as counterintuitive as this idea may seem, it's time everyone should learn that by not playing with fire, we are playing with fire.

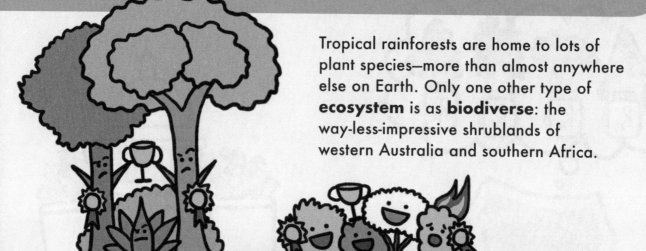

Tropical rainforests are home to lots of plant species—more than almost anywhere else on Earth. Only one other type of **ecosystem** is as **biodiverse**: the way-less-impressive shrublands of western Australia and southern Africa.

Rainforests and shrublands seem very different, but both owe their diversity, in part, to the fact that their soils have very low levels of nitrogen and phosphorus—**nutrients** plants need to grow.

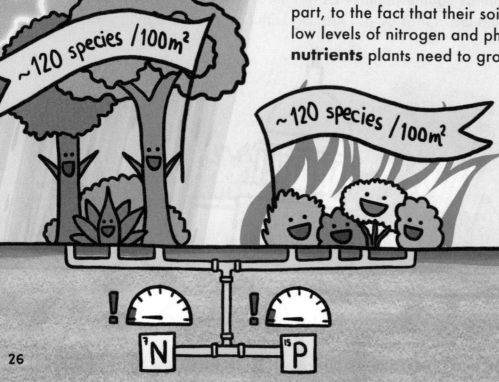

~120 species /100m²

~120 species /100m²

Logically, it seems like richer soils should be better for growing plants. And in ecosystems with lots of soil nutrients, there are plenty of plants, but not plenty of different species.

That's because the species that grow quickly grab most of the nutrients, which lets them keep growing quickly. Their leaves and roots snatch up lots of water and sunlight—so much that slower-growing species can't get enough to survive.

Poor soils, on the other hand, don't provide enough nutrients for fast-growing plants to build massive networks of stems and leaves to hog all the resources. Here, greedy plants don't have an advantage, so everyone just scrabbles by.

But crummy soil isn't the only thing that encourages super-diversity. For example, beaches and mountaintops have poor soils AND few plant species.

That's because on most of the planet, glaciers regularly bulldoze away entire ecosystems, leaving them to start over from scratch.

Next glaciation in 21,000 years

However, rainforests and shrublands have spent millions of years beyond the reach of glaciers. Their residents have had plenty of undisturbed time to evolve strategies for surviving poor soils. In wet places, those strategies have led to tall, diverse rainforests, and in dry places, they have led to scrubby, diverse shrublands. That's why the poorest places on Earth are actually also the richest.

Why are orchids so successful?

The flowering plants known as orchids are beautiful—and they're also everywhere! Orchids thrive all over the planet, from sub-Antarctic islands to tropical rainforests. They have become so successful by using some very selfish strategies.

For one, while most flowering plants send their seeds off with a supply of nutrients to get them growing, orchids don't.

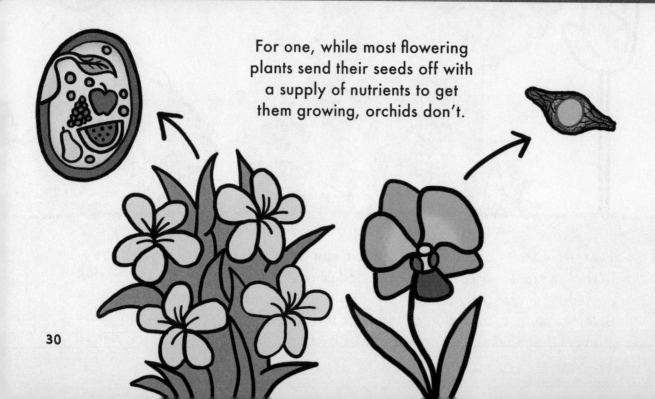

Instead, their seedlings trick **fungi** into feeding them until they're old enough to make their own food through photosynthesis.

Some species trick their fungal partners into life-long one-way relationships. In fact, several are such dedicated moochers that they've lost their sugar-making machinery altogether.

And while most flowers offer snacks to the critters who transfer their **pollen**, orchids cheat their **pollinators** instead.

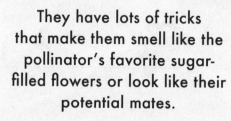

They have lots of tricks that make them smell like the pollinator's favorite sugar-filled flowers or look like their potential mates.

For example, an Australian hammer orchid looks and smells like a flightless female wasp. But when a male wasp tries to carry her off to mate, he instead catapults right into the flower, where he'll pick up a sticky packet of pollen.

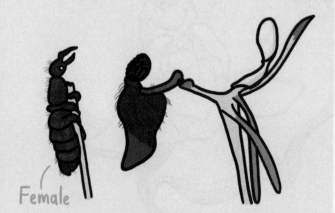

Female

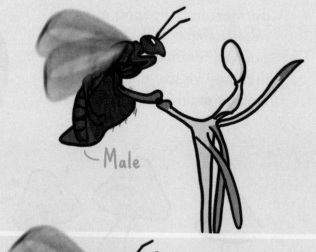

Male

Pollen

Orchids may all share these greedy strategies, but as a group, they are very diverse. Each species is highly adapted for its particular **habitat**—that's why there are more than 25,000 different species of orchids!

They're so customized that if you were to dig one up and replant it ten meters away, it might not survive. So orchids don't just look special—they're also amazing specialists.

Can plants talk?

Compared to the ruckus animals can make, plants seem like the silent type. But just because they're quiet doesn't mean they aren't communicating.

When they're under attack, some plants—like corn and cotton—summon animals as defenders. They emit chemical compounds that attract **parasitic** wasps, which inject their eggs into plant-munching caterpillars so the wasp larvae can eat them from the inside out. Teamwork!

Plants gossip below ground as well. Even if you seal the tops of tomato plants in airtight plastic bags and expose one of them to a harmful leaf disease, the healthy plants will detect their neighbors' illness and begin making antibiotic compounds.

This communication probably happens through the extensive network of beneficial fungi that help plant roots absorb and share water and nutrients.

However, plants can also use what they learn about their neighbors for nastier purposes. Parasitic dodder vines sniff out and steer towards their preferred **hosts** instead of flailing around blindly. Another vine somehow grows leaves of different shapes and sizes to match those of the tree or shrub it's climbing on, using its host for both support and camouflage.

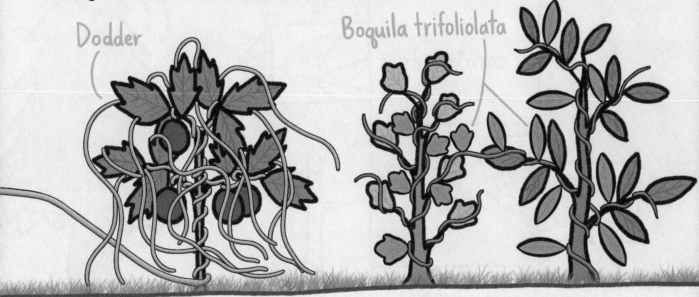

Dodder

Boquila trifoliolata

Whatever the purpose, plants have been chatting and eavesdropping in complex social networks since long before social media or texting.
If anything, we took a leaf from their book.

Why do leaves change color in fall?

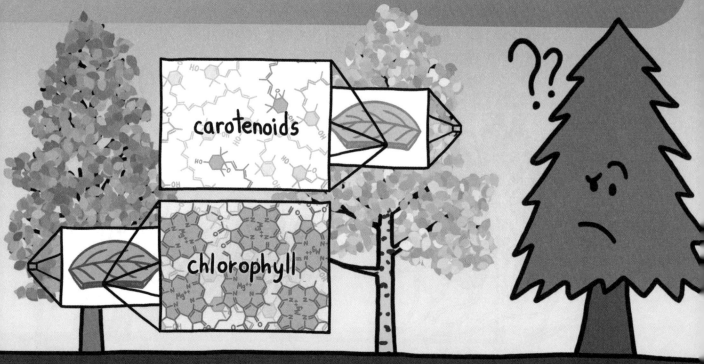

carotenoids

chlorophyll

Evergreen trees like pines stay, well, green all year round. Other trees change colors every fall when their leaves lose their green **chlorophyll** molecules, revealing colorful molecules beneath. But what makes this happen?

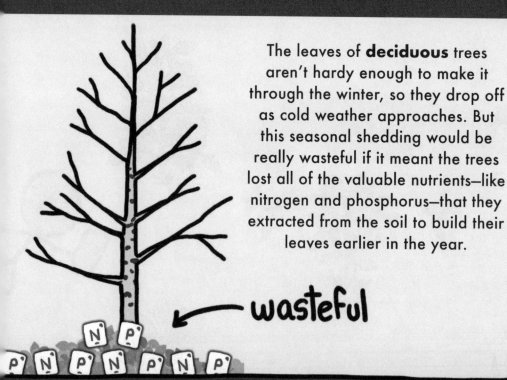

The leaves of **deciduous** trees aren't hardy enough to make it through the winter, so they drop off as cold weather approaches. But this seasonal shedding would be really wasteful if it meant the trees lost all of the valuable nutrients—like nitrogen and phosphorus—that they extracted from the soil to build their leaves earlier in the year.

wasteful

So each fall, deciduous trees recycle those nutrients.

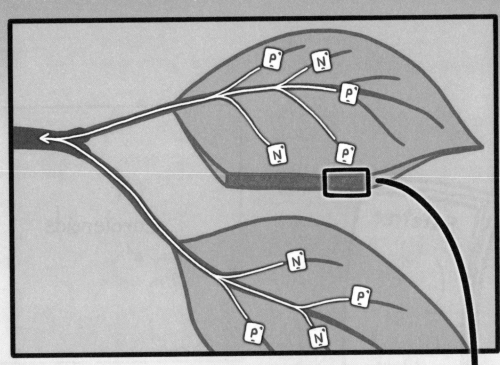

That involves taking apart cells and photosynthetic machinery in order to get the nutrients out of the leaves and store them in twigs and branches until next spring.

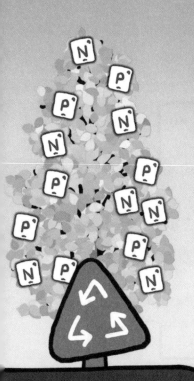

This is actually really tricky, because as the disassembly starts, chlorophyll molecules are still absorbing the sun's energy. But with no photosynthesis happening, they pass the unused energy along to oxygen molecules, which become dangerously reactive and wreak havoc in the leaf.

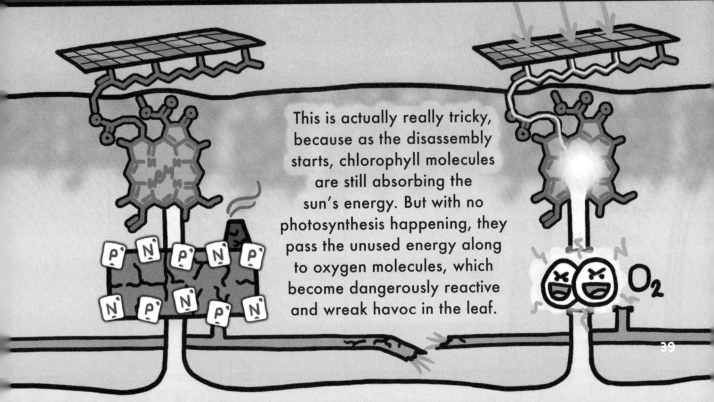

O_2

To keep the destruction to a minimum, leaves break down their chlorophyll into less dangerous molecules that are typically transparent. With the bright green molecules gone, yellow and orange pigments that were there all along are no longer overshadowed, and ta-da: yellow and orange leaves!

Safetree

Chlorophyll catabolites

Carotenoids

Some trees take another precaution against chlorophyll-induced destruction: as the dismantling starts, they build new pigments to shade chlorophyll from sunlight until it can be broken down. These new pigments tend to be red, so trees that use them have red leaves in the fall.

EXTRA Safetree

Anthocyanins

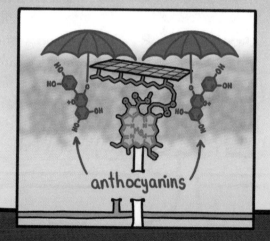

anthocyanins

These colorful displays help deciduous trees recover as much as half of the nitrogen and phosphorus from their old leaves to help grow fresh new green ones in the spring. Deciduous trees are perhaps the world's prettiest recycling plants.

Who are flowers trying to seduce?

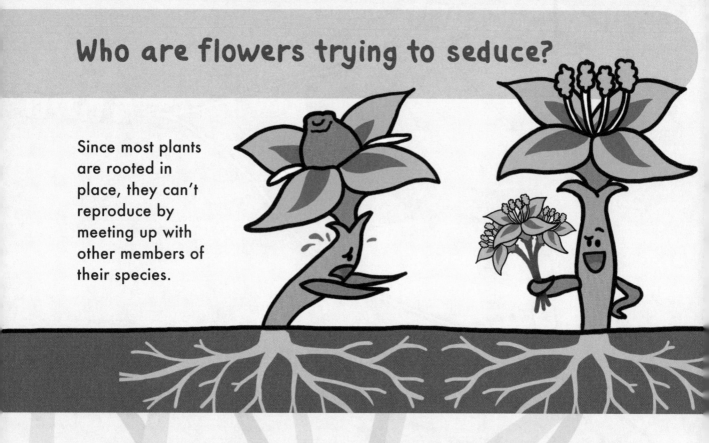

Since most plants are rooted in place, they can't reproduce by meeting up with other members of their species.

Instead, they rely on outside forces to transport their pollen from male flower parts to female ones—and they're tailor-made for their preferred pollinator.

For example, the yellows and blues of certain flowers match up with the colors that a bee can see best.

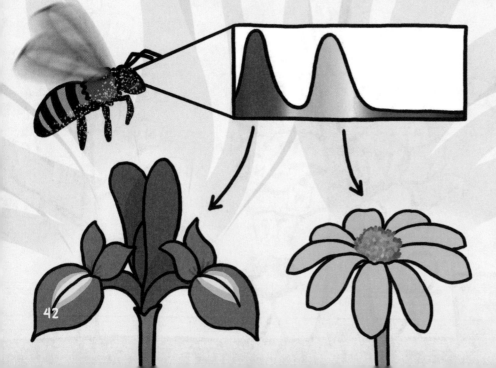

And because bees are stellar smellers, these flowers also spritz out tempting perfume.

Many bee-pollinated plants also offer convenient, ultraviolet-marked landing pads where the pudgy insects can rest.

Hummingbirds have a lousy sense of smell but an excellent memory, so flowers that cater to them are scentless, but churn out sweet nectar to keep them coming back. These flowers are often red to keep their nectar safe from red-blind bees, who might otherwise snag the sugary reward without picking up pollen.

Other flowers bloom at night, bearing bright-white petals and strong smells that draw moths and bats in the dark.

Still others give off the smell of dead meat to attract scavenging flies.

And some plants grow close to the ground and emit a yeasty scent to lure in rodent pollinators.

Of course, many plants have multiple pollinators, and most pollinators tend to more than one kind of plant. But almost every plant is continuously evolving to maximize its pollination potential, and as a result, their flowers hint at who—or what—moves most of their pollen.

Because for plants, "the birds and the bees" really is all about birds and the bees—and the flies, moths, butterflies, bats, rodents, and more.

Why are fish getting smaller?

For most of the species that we fish, we are only allowed to keep individuals above a minimum size.

Legal

The idea behind these laws is to make sure young fish can grow big enough to reproduce at least once before becoming our dinner.

In theory, that means there will always be enough fish for dinner tomorrow.

Except, it doesn't really work.

We're basically breeding smaller fish, unintentionally; heavily-fished fish are now about half the weight they were 40 years ago. Six-year-old haddock, for example, now weigh 40% of what they did in 1970—that's like full-grown men weighing 65 pounds!

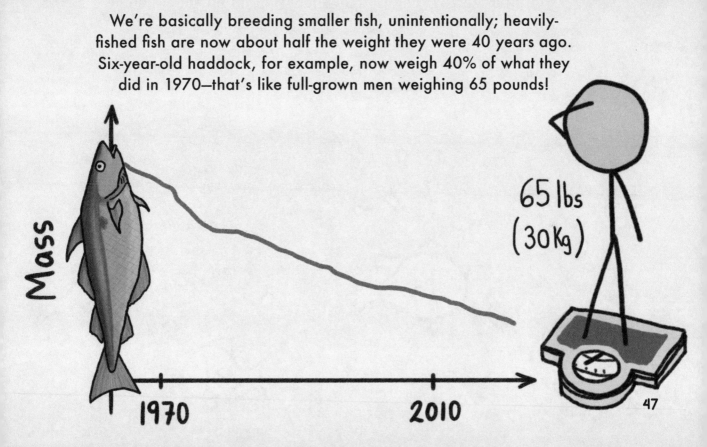

Large fish are better at making successful offspring than small fish both because they produce more eggs and because their eggs contain more food for the babies growing inside. So by removing the largest fish of a given species, we make it harder for the population to replenish itself.

Plus, if we are always removing the biggest fish, only the fish that are naturally small for their age will live long enough to make babies. These small fish pass on their small-fish **genes** to new generations, while big fish and their big-fish genes become rarer and rarer.

48

Here's a better idea: instead of reeling in all the largest individuals, we should catch a smaller number of fish across a wider range of sizes to keep the numbers and sizes of fish balanced.

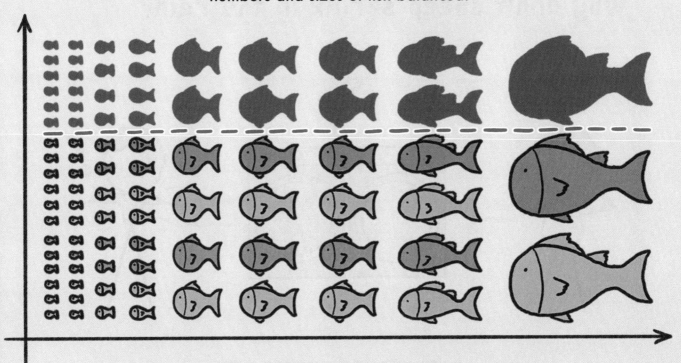

Sooner rather than later, we'll have to accept that it's good to let some of the big ones get away. That way, we can make sure there are plenty of fish in the sea.

Why don't sheep shrink in the rain?

If you put a wool sweater through
the laundry, it shrinks. So why don't
sheep—which are basically made of
wool—shrink when they get wet?
The answer comes down to **friction**.

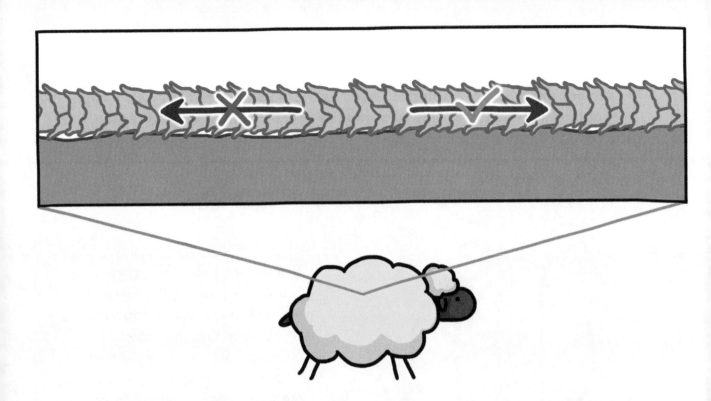

Like all **mammal** hair, wool fibers are covered in overlapping scales, which make it easier for the fiber to slide in one direction than the other.

That's why, if you pull a strand of your own hair through your fingers, the motion is much smoother as you move toward the tip than toward the root.

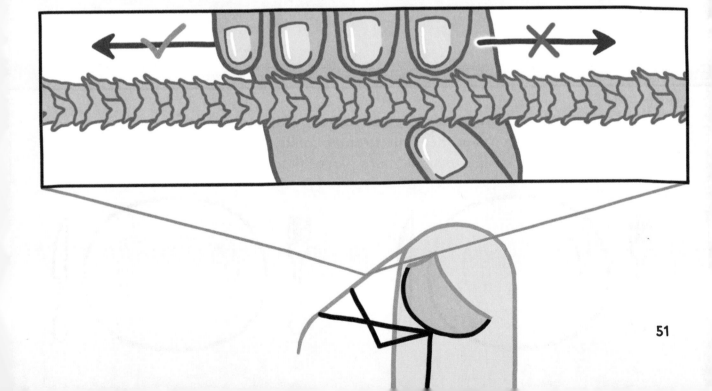

When a wool sweater goes into the washing machine and gets tossed around, this one-way resistance becomes a problem. Each fiber gets caught against its neighbors, only allowing the fibers to move in one direction.

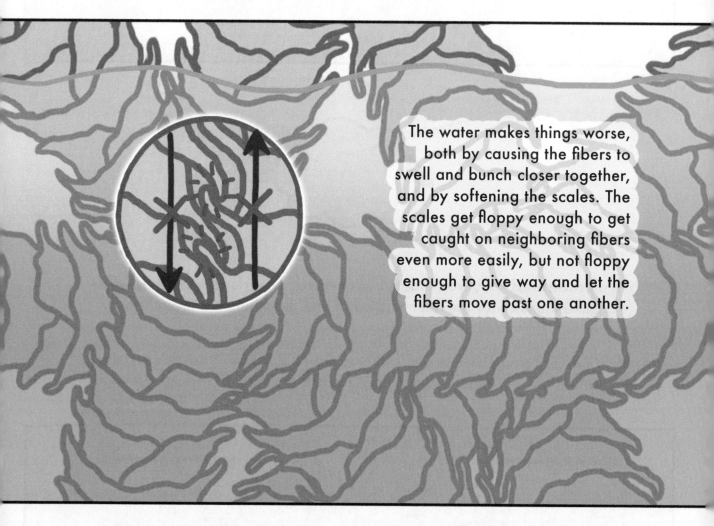

The water makes things worse, both by causing the fibers to swell and bunch closer together, and by softening the scales. The scales get floppy enough to get caught on neighboring fibers even more easily, but not floppy enough to give way and let the fibers move past one another.

Heat also makes the friction problem worse. It makes the fibers more bendy, which brings them into greater contact—the same way cooked spaghetti noodles touch in more places than hard, uncooked ones.

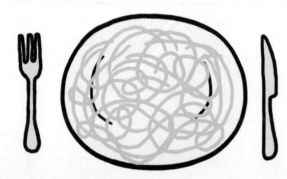

Throughout the wash and dry cycle, the millions of tiny scales on the thousands of individual fibers in the wool sweater draw the fabric more and more tightly together, shrinking the overall size of the sweater.

When sheep get caught in the rain, the fibers in their thick coats swell and their scales soften, but their wool doesn't get tossed around enough to shrink...unless those sheep get really RAM-bunctious.

How did whales get so big?

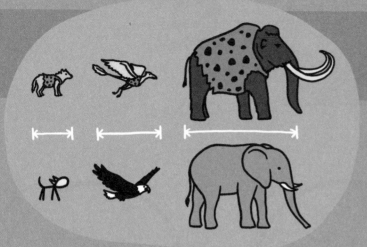

Animals come in all different sizes, but most of them stay about the same size over evolutionary time.

That's because as an animal gets bigger, it gets a little bit stronger, but a LOT heavier, and eventually it can no longer lug around its own weight.

However, once in a while, a series of lucky breaks allows an animal to get truly gigantic...

When whales' land-dwelling predecessors plunged back into the ocean, the water could carry their weight, so the critters could grow way bigger without worrying about holding up their massive bodies.

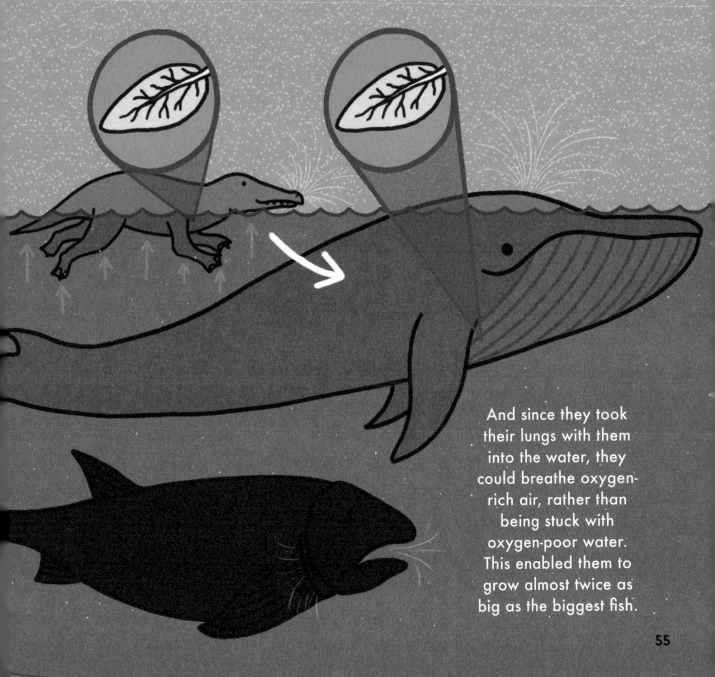

And since they took their lungs with them into the water, they could breathe oxygen-rich air, rather than being stuck with oxygen-poor water. This enabled them to grow almost twice as big as the biggest fish.

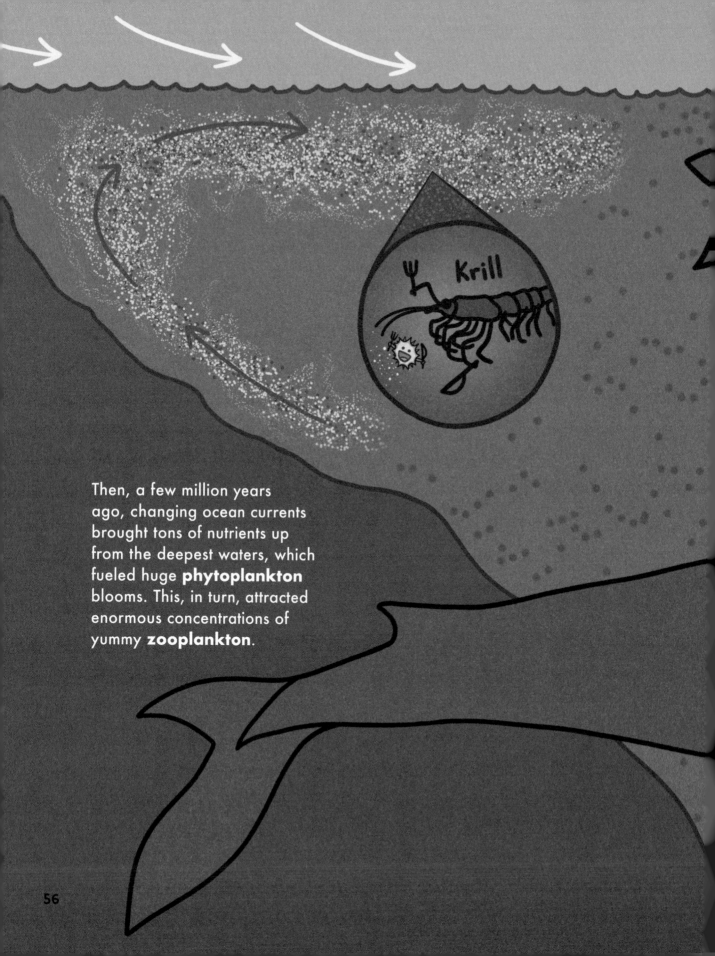

Krill

Then, a few million years ago, changing ocean currents brought tons of nutrients up from the deepest waters, which fueled huge **phytoplankton** blooms. This, in turn, attracted enormous concentrations of yummy **zooplankton**.

3 MILLION YEARS AGO

With this new krillion-calorie diet, blue whales quickly became the largest animals to have ever lived. And THAT is certainly something to spout about!

TODAY

Which of these is a bee?

When you imagine a bee, you probably think of something like this.

wasp

bee

But bee-lieve it or not, most bee species don't have yellow and black stripes. And there are lots of yellow-and-black-striped insects that are not actually bees. This confusion actually has a purpose—it's a tactic that tells predators to buzz off.

moth

fly

bee

bee

Insects that can make nasty defensive chemicals or can sting are often brightly colored, so predators learn to keep their distance.

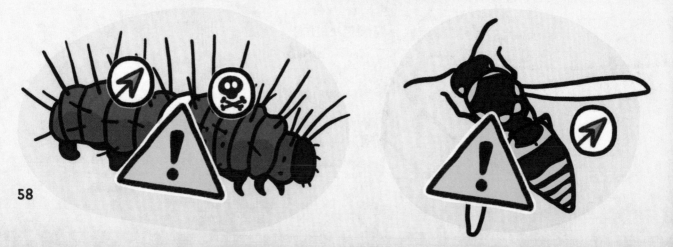

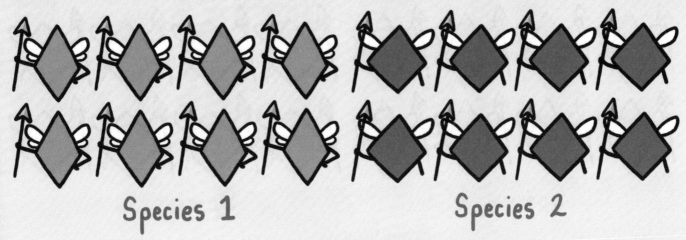

Species 1   Species 2

Predator

If two stinging species have different warning colorations; a
predator must sample lots of each kind before learning that
both patterns yield un-happy meals.

Species 1   Species 2

Predator

But if the two species look similar, far fewer of each kind will get chomped before the predator learns to avoid that pattern.

So stinging species, like bees and wasps, often end up converging on a similar appearance.

Once predators learn that yellow-and-black-striped prey isn't worth the risk, cheaters creep into the system. Neither flies nor moths have stingers for defense, but simply looking like an insect that does have a stinger provides pretty much the same protection.

fly

moth

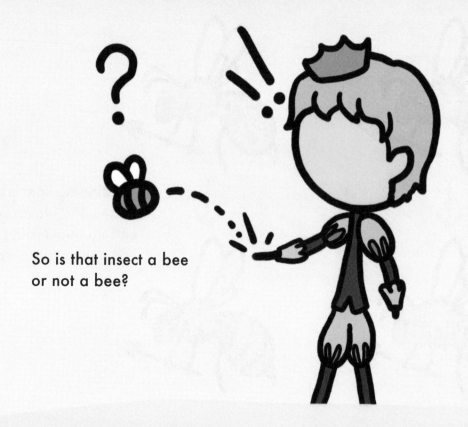

So is that insect a bee or not a bee?

If it just stung you, it's a bee or a wasp. Along with stingers, both have short, elbow-shaped antennae and four wings—although those can be hard to see. Bees are the super-hairy ones, while wasps are mostly bald.

wasp

bee

On the non-stinging side, if it has two wings and looks like it's wearing giant goggles, it's a fly. If it has long, feathery antennae, it's probably a moth.

If you can get beyond the fear of getting stung and begin to appreciate their differences, you may find that beauty is in the eye of the bee-holder.

Why don't migrating birds take the shortest route?

Each fall, billions of birds migrate to the tropics. But instead of flying straight, they often zig and zag along the way.

These detours can add more than a thousand miles to the birds' journeys, but they actually help the birds get to their destinations faster.

12 000 km!

9600 km

Birds that fly with the wind at least partially at their backs can fly a lot faster than those that fly against the wind.

So even if, say, a swallow has to fly 25% farther to take advantage of the wind, if it doubles its airspeed velocity by doing so, it can get there in less than two thirds the time.

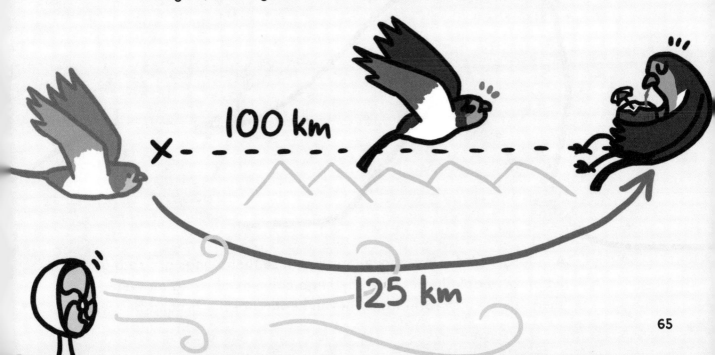

100 km

125 km

All these detours cause birds
from all over the world to gather
at a few key **land bridges**.

For a few weeks each year, these hotspots
fill with flocks of squawking foreigners—both
in the sky and on the ground below.

Does it really make sense to mate for life?

Monogamy—the practice of mating with a single individual for an extended period of time—isn't that popular in the animal kingdom.

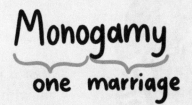

Monogamy
one marriage

3%.   95%.

Only about 3% of mammals are monogamous, and although 95% of birds pair off (at least for a while), paternity tests show that the avian world is chock-full of cheaters.

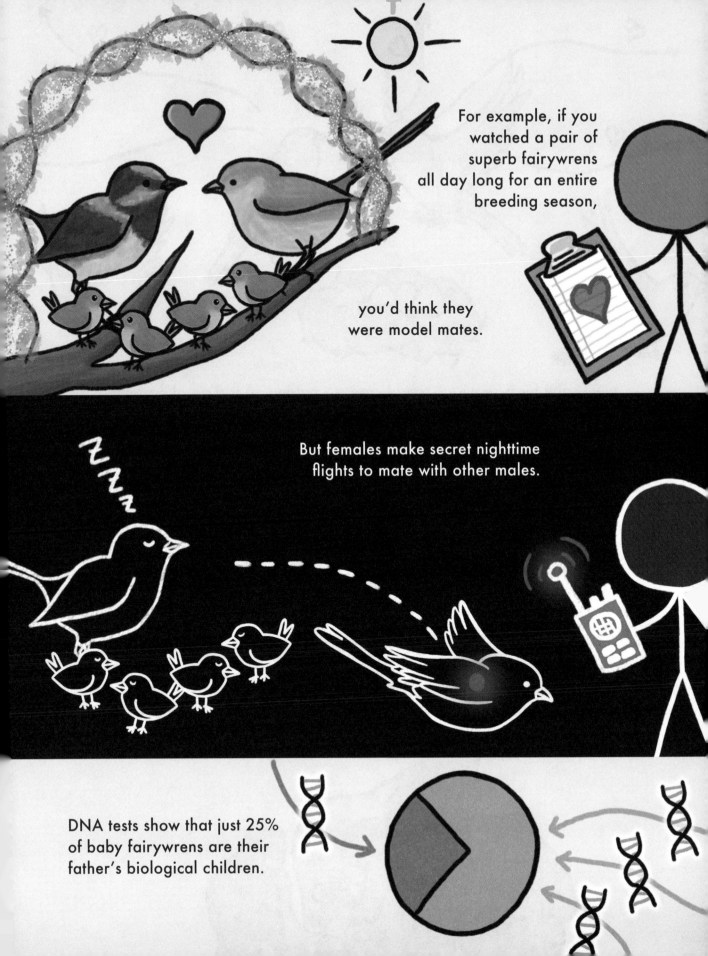

For example, if you watched a pair of superb fairywrens all day long for an entire breeding season,

you'd think they were model mates.

But females make secret nighttime flights to mate with other males.

DNA tests show that just 25% of baby fairywrens are their father's biological children.

Baby birds require a ton of care, so pairing up is a good parenting strategy. But it also makes sense for each partner to sneak in some genetic variety—hence the female fairywrens' secret flights.

Cheating can explain why males and females in supposedly-monogamous species sometimes look so unexpectedly different. We've long known that the less monogamous a species is, the more different its two sexes tend to look.

That's because the traits that help one sex get—and defend—all those mates often become more and more pronounced over the generations; think of giant antlers or a broad silver back.

One thing is clear: among all the species on Earth, true monogamy is rare. There is, however, at least one known example of a perfect lifelong pairing:

Diplozoon paradoxum

These flatworms literally fuse together to form what looks like a single organism, and the union lasts for their entire lives, which they spend sucking blood from fish gills...a truly romantic attachment.

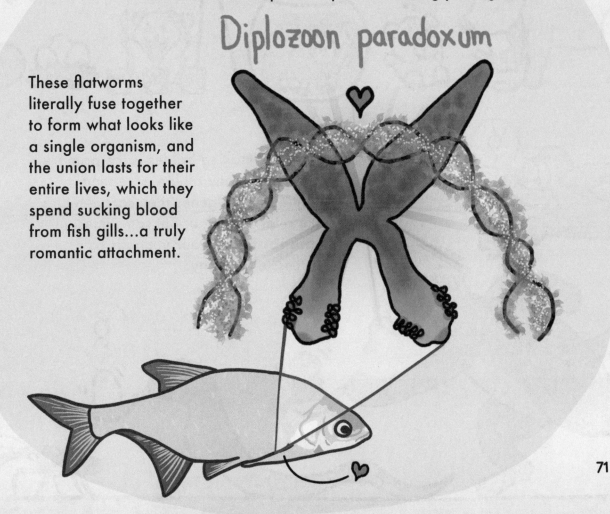

71

Why do some animals eat their babies?

Lots of animals, from fish to birds to primates, all occasionally nom on their own babies...which is distressing and weird.

XI
THOU SHALL NOT EAT THINE OWN BABIES

After all, making babies is the primary goal of virtually all life, so eating them—and the genes they carry—seems like a terrible idea. But sometimes, **cannibalizing** your young is a successful strategy.

For instance, hamsters seem to use baby-eating as crowd control. Females with litters of eight or nine pups eat, on average, two of them.

When scientists add pups to the litter, the hamster moms eat four.

But removing a few pups the day they're born stops the cannibalism, suggesting that these moms are trying to keep their litters small enough to be able to provide for the survivors to ensure they grow up to pass on their genes.

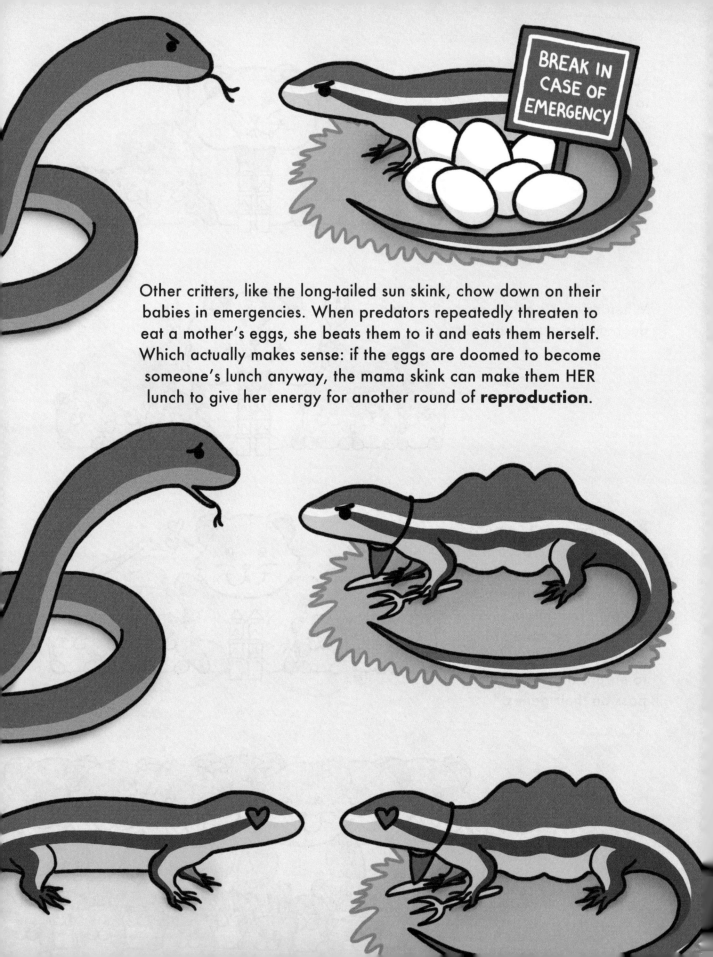

Other critters, like the long-tailed sun skink, chow down on their babies in emergencies. When predators repeatedly threaten to eat a mother's eggs, she beats them to it and eats them herself. Which actually makes sense: if the eggs are doomed to become someone's lunch anyway, the mama skink can make them HER lunch to give her energy for another round of **reproduction**.

BREAK IN CASE OF EMERGENCY

And sometimes, kids just get in the way. The male sand goby fertilizes eggs from multiple females and cares for them all together in one nest. In order to mate again, he has to wait for all his eggs to hatch, so he sacrifices the slowpokes by eating them to free himself up for more baby-making.

In short, critters across the animal kingdom are just maximizing the resources, energy, and opportunities they need to pass on their genes. So sometimes it does make sense to order off of the kids' menu.

Which plants & animals should we save?

Today, over 20,000 species on Earth are at risk of disappearing, but we don't have enough time or money to save them all. How do we decide where to start?

It's a tough situation, but not a unique one. Medical first responders regularly make decisions like these, and a similar urgency-based approach could help us decide which species to prioritize saving first.

For example, we could save the most **endangered** plants and animals first, like the last few wild Javan rhinos in the world.

Or those with the best chances of long term survival, like Maud Island frogs threatened by invasive species.

Or those that play key roles in their ecosystem:

like mangrove trees, which support over a thousand species,

or otters, whose urchin-eating keeps kelp forests healthy.

But so far, we seem to be saving the cutest species. We donate big bucks to fancy **conservation** campaigns represented by animals like pandas and tigers, and most of this money doesn't get shared with other threatened species.

1864 left

only 60 left

Keeping the spotlight focused on a few celebrities can mean the demise of species with less-adorable faces—or no faces at all. But these underdog species are often ideal conservation candidates: they can be simpler to resuscitate, less expensive to protect, and vital to their ecosystems... their only flaw is that they aren't all that cute.

Should we really let appearances decide who lives and who dies, or should we take a more rational approach?

Perhaps it depends on whether we think a world without species like pandas is something we can bear.

Why is it so hard to get rid of invasive species?

Earth's ecosystems are constantly changing.
But since humans arrived, we've put things into fast-forward,
moving all sorts of organisms around the globe—intentionally or not.

And when a newcomer takes hold and harms us or part of the environment we care about, we call it an "invasive species."

Some invasive species cost us money. The US spends billions of dollars fighting the pretty but pesky yellow rocket flower that chokes fields and creeps onto golf courses.

But even when billions aren't at stake, some invaders wreak so much havoc on fragile ecosystems that we can't help but notice them.

lionfish

The yellow crazy ant, a likely native of Southeast Asia, has been nomming endangered Australian creatures since its arrival. These ants feast on anything in their path: insects, amphibians, birds, mammals...

...even the famous red crabs on Christmas Island, which used to keep the island's undergrowth in check. As a result, the ecosystem has veered into chaos. But noticing invasive species is easy; dealing with them is the real challenge.

When we brought rabbits to New Zealand for food and fur, they bred like...well...rabbits.

We introduced ferrets to control them, but the ferrets ignored the rabbits and gobbled up rare species like the now nearly-extinct kakapo.

New Zealand is still overrun by both furry fiends.

It's better to arm ourselves with knowledge.

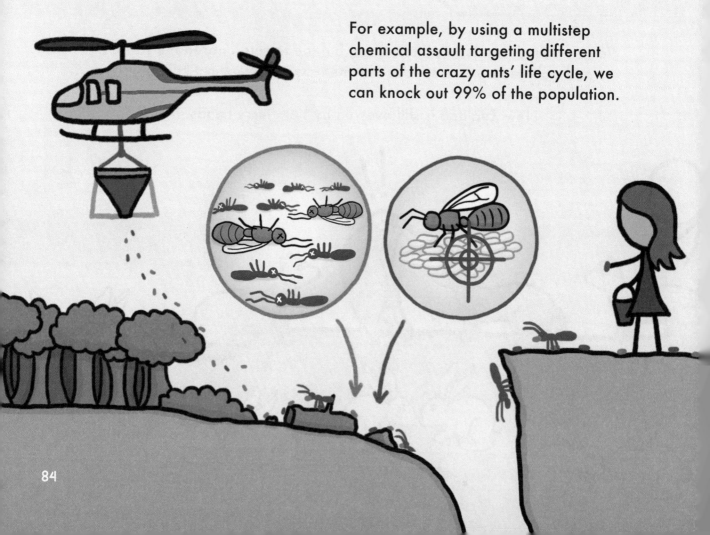

For example, by using a multistep chemical assault targeting different parts of the crazy ants' life cycle, we can knock out 99% of the population.

But even 99% isn't enough for most invaders, because they still have whatever advantage gave them an edge, so they can bounce right back.

We really need to stop moving potential troublemakers around in the first place. In today's globalized world this is easier said than done, but it's our best chance of keeping invasive species' harmful ant-ics at bay.

Why do some species thrive in cities?

As we turn more and more of our real jungles into concrete jungles, we put more and more species at risk. But there are plants and animals that survive—and even thrive—in cities.

Some lucky species happen to be naturally suited to cities. For instance, English ivy and rock pigeons climb and roost on vertical structures like trees and cliffs anyway, so brick walls and sky-high ledges are fine substitutes.

And **omnivorous** raccoons thrive on an urban buffet of everything from corn chips to cockroaches, helping ten times more raccoons pack into a city than a similar-sized woodland habitat.

Natural flexibility can also help animals cope with the stresses of urban living. Coyotes that colonize cities often become more nocturnal to minimize their encounters with humans.

And even if animals aren't naturally adapted to city life, some animals are just more likely to evolve into city slickers than others.

New York City's white-footed mice are one example. These urban dwellers' genes differ from their country cousins' in more than 30 significant ways.

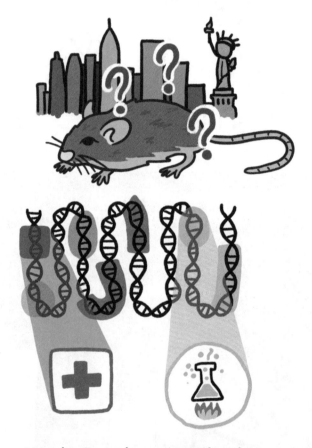

We don't yet know exactly what effects these changes have, but we know they've shown up in genes involved in fighting disease and processing **toxins**—traits that likely help mice survive in crowded conditions.

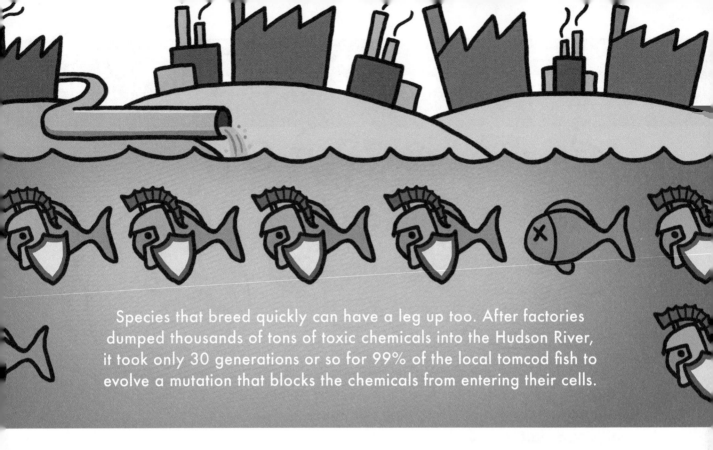

Species that breed quickly can have a leg up too. After factories dumped thousands of tons of toxic chemicals into the Hudson River, it took only 30 generations or so for 99% of the local tomcod fish to evolve a mutation that blocks the chemicals from entering their cells.

This doesn't mean that cities are a boon for biodiversity, but they aren't biological dead zones either—they're more like accidental laboratories where the limits of life's adjustability are being tested...and tasted.

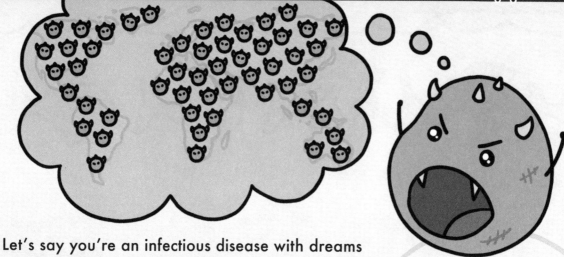

Let's say you're an infectious disease with dreams of spreading far and wide. A logical starting point would be to invade a host and make as many mini-yous as fast as you can to spread to as many other hosts as you can.

However, that would probably be a bad idea, because the more of yourself you make, the worse your host feels. And the worse they feel, the less likely they are to go out and interact with other potential hosts.

That's a problem if you're like most **pathogens** and require close contact—like a handshake or a shared drink—to move from host to host. Most diseases have to limit the damage they cause, so that their hosts feel well enough to drag themselves out of bed and into contact with other potential hosts.

But if a pathogen can get passed along without close contact, it is free to get really nasty. The diarrhea-causing bacteria that causes cholera can kill its hosts in just a few hours. Since the disease can move through water, hosts don't have to be particularly mobile to transmit it. In fact, sicker hosts poop more bacteria into the water supply, infecting even more people.

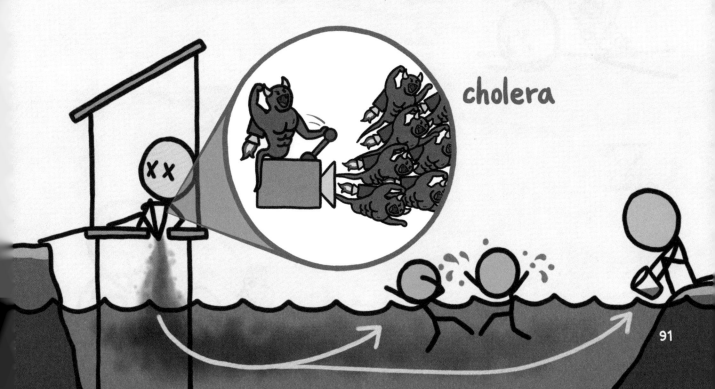

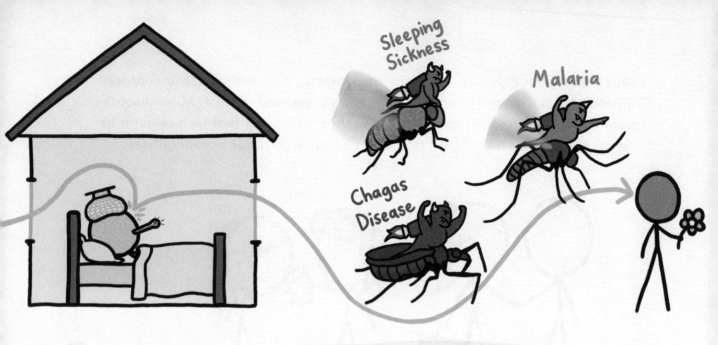

Sleeping Sickness

Malaria

Chagas Disease

The same is true for diseases transmitted by flies, mosquitoes, and other creepy-crawlies, which can access even super-sick hosts and spread the pathogen around, and for diseases like anthrax, which can linger in the environment for years waiting for a new host.

Anthrax

In general, pathogens that can be passed along at a distance—or after long periods of time—tend to be more lethal than those that require close contact.

Pathogens, of course, don't actually strategize for world domination. But nature is constantly selecting for strategies that work, and that means pushing some diseases to mildness and others toward knock-down, drag-out devastation.

How much food is there on Earth?

Canada's Quebec province produces almost three-quarters of the world's maple syrup, and hoards 50,000 barrels of it. Other countries have food reserves too, both for economic and emergency reasons.

If something terrible were to happen, how long could humanity get by on the food we have in the planet's cupboards, supermarkets, warehouses, and silos?

The short answer is: not very long. Grains like corn, rice, and wheat, and tubers like potatoes and cassava make up most of our food stores, and on their own, they could feed humanity for about three months.

Add in everything else we have stored up—fruits and vegetables, meat, milk, eggs, oil, and sugar—and we could extend our rations by another four weeks... and that would be it.

However, there is a lot of *potential* food out there.

If we picked all the berries and mushrooms in the world, they'd feed humanity for another hour or two.

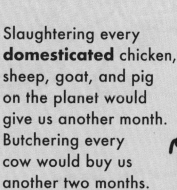

Hunting the world's wild mammals and birds would get us by for a few days.

Slaughtering every **domesticated** chicken, sheep, goat, and pig on the planet would give us another month. Butchering every cow would buy us another two months.

If we caught all the fish, shrimp, crab, and krill in the ocean, they would sustain us for about six months.

And if we could vacuum up all the termites, ants, and earthworms in the entire world, they'd feed us for another six months.

Eating all of Earth's animals, plus all of our stored food, probably shouldn't be our first plan, but hypothetically, we'd have enough calories to feed us for around a year and a half.

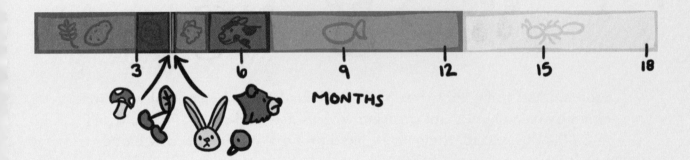

MONTHS

And that maple syrup? Each person would get half a teaspoon—almost enough to sweeten a couple of termites.

How is milk REALLY made?

Supermarkets today have lots of different kinds of milk, many of which are made by blending up and straining various nuts and seeds. Plain old milk, on the other hand, is also a strained product—it's filtered cow blood.

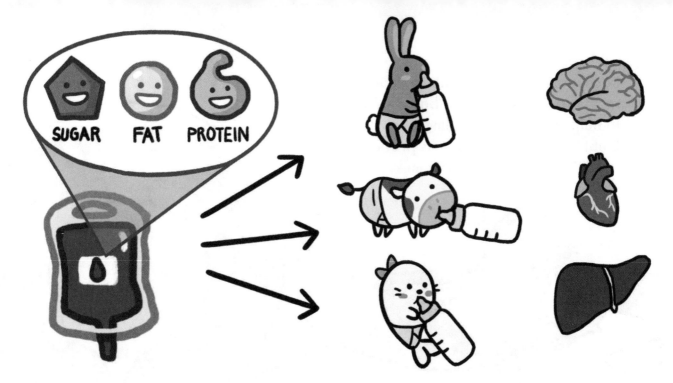

As weird as this seems, it makes sense because blood contains lots of sugar, fat, and protein—exactly what baby mammals need to grow complex brains and bodies. But mammal mamas can't just open an artery; that would be dangerous. Plus, most of the nutrients in blood aren't concentrated enough to be useful.

This is where the mammary gland comes in. It's full of thousands of tiny sacs whose walls have special cells that grab water and nutrients from passing blood, do some fancy chemistry on them, and pass them into the sacs. There, they combine to become the final milky mixture.

Each mammal species tailors its blood-filtering recipe to the needs of its babies. For example, to help their Arctic-dwelling pups pack on the blubber, hooded seal moms produce milk that is 15 times fattier than cow milk.

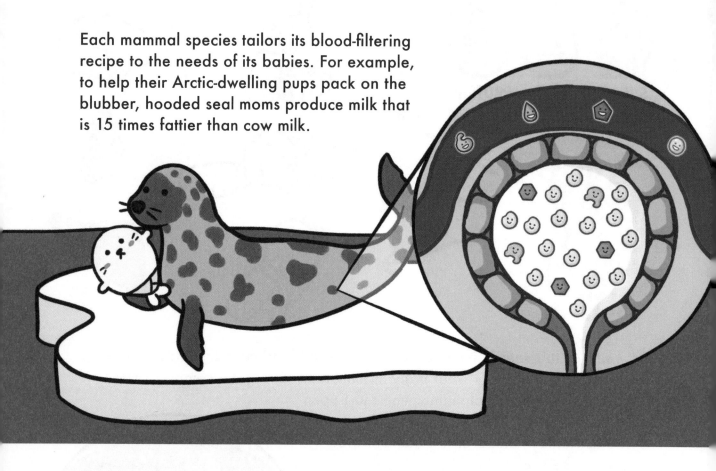

Cottontail moms make high-protein milk for their bunny babies, allowing them to develop their hopping muscles quickly.

The tammar wallaby can make two different types of milk in two different teats at the same time: one high in sugars for a newborn in the pouch, and one high in fat and protein for her older offspring.

And while modern dairy cows don't have a particularly wacky recipe for their milk, they sure make a lot of it. The current record holder—a cow named "Aftershock"—can produce a bathtub full of milk every day...that's udderly impressive.

Why do we eat spoiled foods?

Some of humans' favorite foods, like coffee, bread, cheese, beer—even chocolate—are home to millions of **microbes**.

That might seem gross, but these foods only get the tastes, smells, and textures we love because of tiny bacteria and fungi.

For example, microbes called "yeast" gorge on the sugary starch in bread dough, then burp out carbon dioxide that helps give loaves their lift.

And bacteria and fungi take turns munching on piles of cacao beans, mellowing out bitter polyphenol molecules and helping create the complex and delicious taste of chocolate.

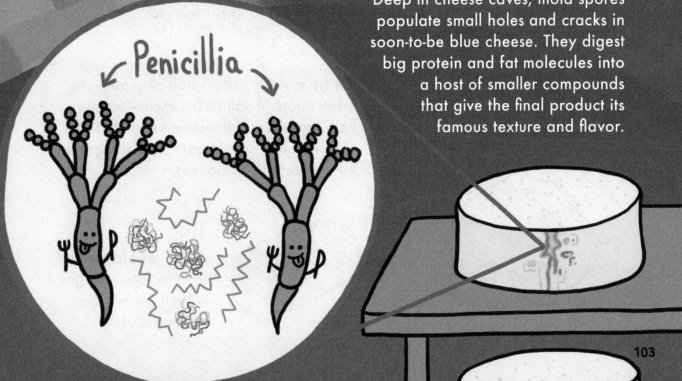

Deep in cheese caves, mold spores populate small holes and cracks in soon-to-be blue cheese. They digest big protein and fat molecules into a host of smaller compounds that give the final product its famous texture and flavor.

Penicillia

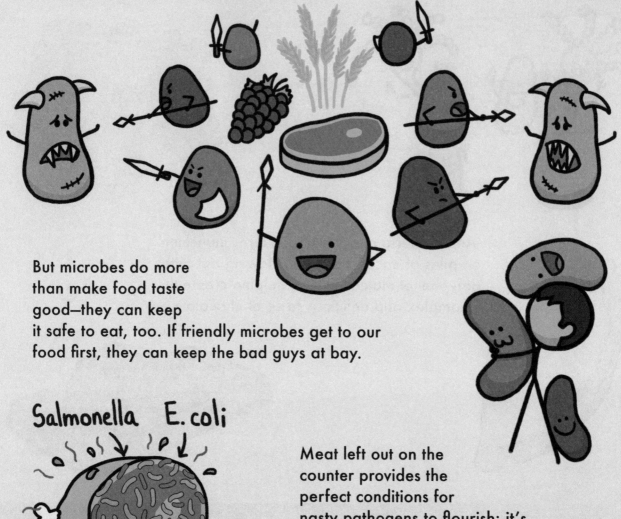

But microbes do more than make food taste good—they can keep it safe to eat, too. If friendly microbes get to our food first, they can keep the bad guys at bay.

Salmonella   E.coli

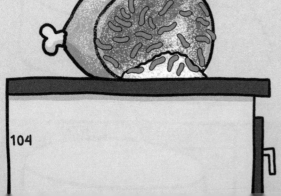

Meat left out on the counter provides the perfect conditions for nasty pathogens to flourish: it's warm, moist, and protein-rich.

But by making some small changes—like adding lots of salt to the meat—we can help harmless, salt-tolerant microbes like *Lactobacillus* outcompete their dangerous but salt-sensitive relatives.

Lactobacillus

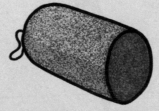

A few unrefrigerated months later, we get salami, rather than *Salmonella*!

Our ancestors stumbled on this kind of controlled spoilage thousands of years ago—either by lucky accidents or out of desperation—and humans around the world have been intentionally spoiling our food ever since.

Cheers!

Where did our food originally come from?

Apple pie is a famous symbol of America—but none of the ingredients in apple pie are originally from the US.

Apples were domesticated somewhere around Kazakhstan, wheat and butter originated in the Middle East, eggs came from the jungles around India, lemons originated in Southeast Asia, cinnamon came from China, and nutmeg and sugar were domesticated somewhere around New Guinea.

And Asia's spicy dishes, from India's curries all the way to Korea's kimchis, owe their heat to chiles domesticated in Central America, which got the rice for its rice and beans from Asia.

In fact, an average of two-thirds of the calories consumed in each country come from crops or animals domesticated far away.

That's because most globally-important plants and animals were domesticated in warm, biodiverse regions where humans have lived for a long time, like North Africa, the Middle East, and Asia.

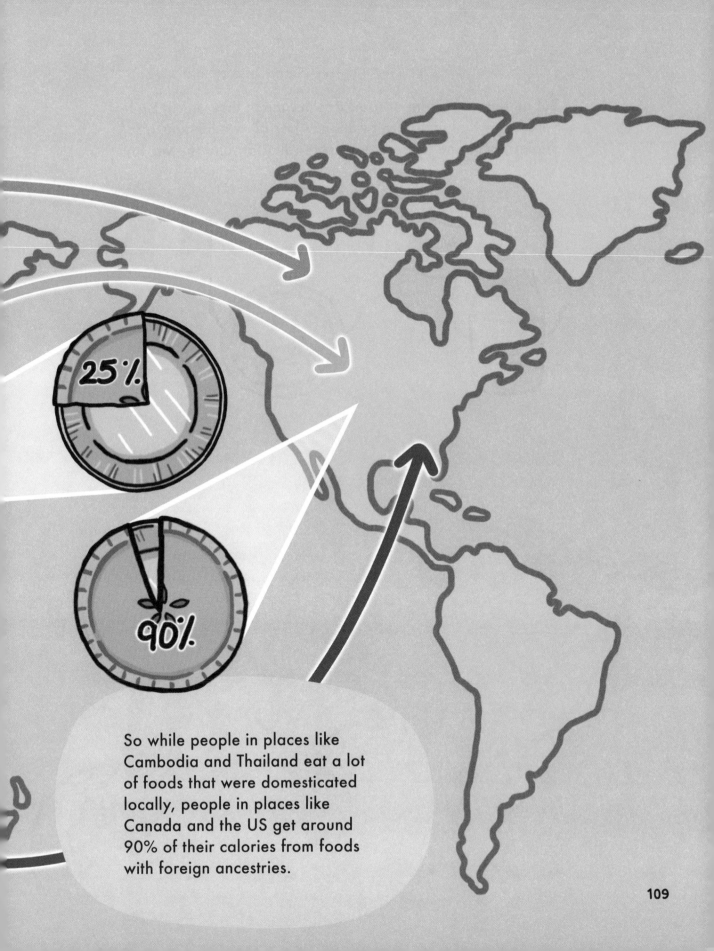

25%.

90%.

So while people in places like Cambodia and Thailand eat a lot of foods that were domesticated locally, people in places like Canada and the US get around 90% of their calories from foods with foreign ancestries.

But all this movement of food doesn't mean that kimchi isn't Korean, or that pizza isn't Italian. After all, we humans also originated in one place before spreading around the world.

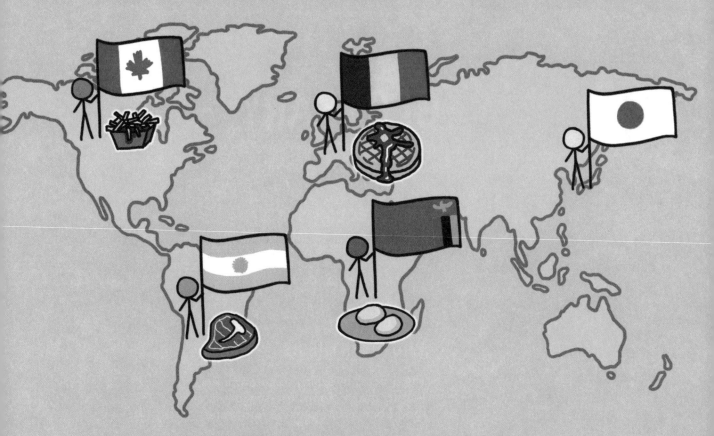

And most of us identify ourselves, and the dishes
we eat, with the places we've ended up.

We say we're Italian, or Indian, or American...
as American, perhaps, as apple pie.

GLOSSARY

INNER SOLAR SYSTEM

The central part of our solar system, which contains the four planets closest to the sun (Mercury, Venus, Earth, and Mars).

PHOTOSYNTHESIS

The process by which some organisms (mostly green plants) use sunlight to make food from carbon dioxide and water.

METEOROID

A small lump of rock traveling through outer space. Most meteoroids are tiny, but some are as large as a meter wide (anything larger is considered an "asteroid").

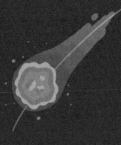

COMET

A ball of ice, dust, and gas that orbits the sun, generally in the farthest part of the solar system.

METEORITE

A meteoroid that survives a trip through the atmosphere and hits the surface of a planet or moon.

ANGIOSPERM

A plant that flowers and produces its seeds within fruits. Plants which do not flower, and produce "naked" seeds (like those in pinecones) are called "gymnosperms."

ECOSYSTEM

A community of living things (like plants, animals, and microbes) and non-living things (like the landscape, weather, and air) that work together and interact with each other.

BIODIVERSE

A term referring to a system containing lots of different species.

NUTRIENT

A substance used by an organism to survive, grow, and reproduce.

FUNGI

A kingdom of organisms that are neither animals or plants. Fungi include yeasts, molds, mushrooms, and other living things that are often good at breaking down material in an ecosystem.

POLLEN

The tiny dust-like grains inside a flowering plant that make it possible for the plant to reproduce.

POLLINATOR

An animal that carries pollen from one flower to another, such as a bee, moth, or bird.

HABITAT

The place where an organism lives, including the natural resources it needs to survive (like food, water, shelter, and space).

PARASITIC

A term used to describe an organism that gets food and shelter from living on or in another living thing, which is harmed in the process.

HOST

A living thing that shelters or provides food for a smaller organism. In a parasitic relationship, the host is harmed by the parasite.

CHLOROPHYLL

A green substance in plants, algae, and some other organisms that absorbs sunlight for use in photosynthesis.

DECIDUOUS

A term used to describe trees and shrubs that shed their leaves at the end of their growing season (usually in autumn).

GENE

A piece of information (made of DNA) that helps determine how a living thing looks and functions, and can be passed from parents to offspring.

FRICTION

The resistance that is created when two objects rub against each other.

MAMMAL

A warm-blooded animal with a backbone and hair or fur. Female mammals make milk to feed their babies.

PHYTOPLANKTON

A diverse group of microscopic plant-like organisms (including algae) that live in water and use photosynthesis to make energy.

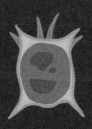

ZOOPLANKTON

A diverse group of microscopic animals that live in water.

LAND BRIDGE

A narrow piece of land that connects two larger pieces of land, such as continents.

CANNIBALISM

The process of an animal eating another animal of the same species.

REPRODUCTION

The process through which organisms create offspring.

ENDANGERED

A term used to describe a species at serious risk of going extinct.

CONSERVATION

The practice of protecting living things from going extinct.

OMNIVOROUS

A term used to describe an organism that eats both plants and animals.

TOXIN

A harmful substance created by a living thing. Some plants and animals use toxins to defend themselves or to catch their prey.

PATHOGEN

A microbe (like a virus or bacteria) that can cause a disease.

DOMESTICATED

A term used to describe plants and animals that humans have bred for a specific reason, such as to produce food (like tomatoes), do work (like sheepdogs), or keep as pets (like cats).

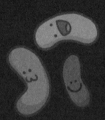

MICROBE

A living thing that is too small to be seen without a microscope.

LEARN MORE!

For lesson plans, further reading, and some of our favorite sources on the subjects in this book, visit:

MinuteEarth.com/Books

ABOUT Minute Earth

The scientists, writers, and illustrators who create MinuteEarth love to ponder all kinds of questions about our planet, no matter whether they are big or small, serious or silly. We also believe that understanding the world around us is one of the best ways to start making a difference. By digging through the scientific literature and talking to all sorts of experts, we create engaging and educational stories that inspire a love for science and an appreciation of our planet.

You can find our short illustrated videos at

Youtube.com/MinuteEarth